THE ABUNDANCE
OF GOD'S LOVE

THE ABUNDANCE OF GOD'S LOVE

FROM LOSS TO LIVING LIFE

Fotina Mugane

Copyright © 2024 by Fotina Mugane

This book is copyright. Except for private study, research, criticism, reviews, or as otherwise permitted under the Australian Copyright Act 1968, no part of this publication may be reproduced or transmitted in any form or by any means without written prior permission from the copyright owner. All inquiries should be made to the author.

No part of this book may be used or reproduced in any manner for the purpose of training artificial intelligence technologies or systems.

Scripture quotations taken from The Holy Bible, New International Version® NIV® Copyright © 1973, 1978, 1984, 2011 by Biblica, Inc. Used by permission. All rights reserved worldwide.

The advice and strategies contained herein may not be suitable for your situation. You should consult with a professional when appropriate. Neither the author nor the editor shall be liable for any loss of profit or any other commercial damages, including but not limited to special, incidental, consequential, personal, or other damages.

Editing and interior design by Empathy Editing

ISBN: 978-0-646-70042-7 (paperback)

ISBN: 978-1-7637118-0-8 (ebook)

 Published by Inspiring Events

 A catalogue record for this book is available from the National Library of Australia

To my son Xavier,
before God formed you, He knew you,
who you were going to become and
who you were going to show up in this world as.
Whatever journey you take,
just know that God is with you and He loves you.

To my amazing family,
thank you for lifting me up,
standing by me, supporting me and
for believing in me when
I couldn't believe in myself.

Thanks to Denise, Liz, Marie and John,
Louisa and John, Cecilia and David, and Cathy and Greg.
You all have shaped me and contributed to my growth
and success in one way or another.
I'm forever indebted to your overwhelming love.

Contents

Introduction   1

Loss   7

Grief   25

Healing   43

Self-Acceptance   59

Living Life   73

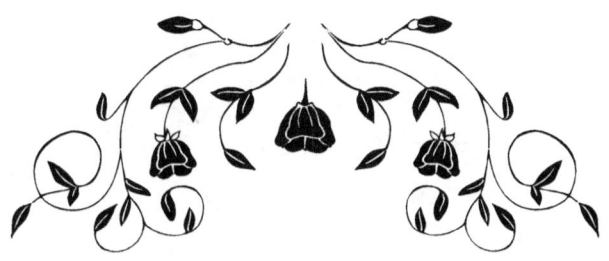

INTRODUCTION

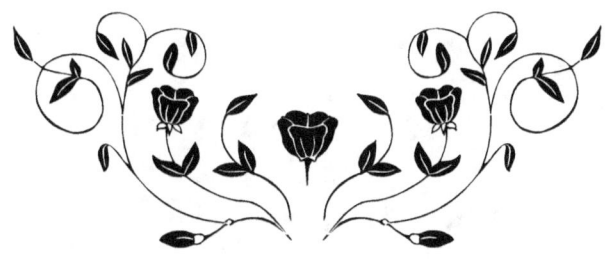

INTRODUCTION

When we talk about God's love, what do we truly mean?

Throughout time, many historic moments have revealed the love of God. We know of His love through the many miracles and wonders that have been witnessed. Yet many are the times we are struck with doubt, wondering if God truly exists. And we ask questions such as: *If He loves me, why does He let things like this happen to me? Where was He when I was going through depression, loss, anxiety, rejection or abandonment?*

These are common thoughts that we believers and individuals go through. What we may forget is a certain flaw of being human: that we carry pre-

NOTES

conceived ideas of who God is and how we expect Him to treat us and show us His love. This limits us from experiencing the ultimate abundance of God's love.

This book challenges us to have a deeper understanding of God's love and explores how to see it during life's trials. To do this, I will take you on a journey through some imagined examples and some lived experiences that have occurred to me or individuals around me.

Although I have written this book in your hands, I am still learning, still growing and still evolving as a person and in my Christian life. As they say, we never stop learning as long as we live; so while much of God and His great love is yet to be revealed to me, in this book I will share the incredible, abundant nature of His love that I found in the darkest of times.

NOTES

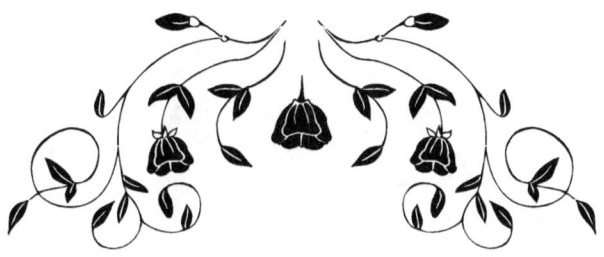

LOSS

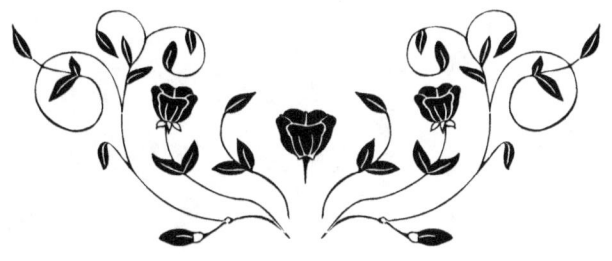

Traditionally many African cultures and other cultures around the world recognise 'rites of passage'. The 'rites' we all experience include some family traditions, from little ones such as who sits where and who says grace to bigger ones such as sharing a Christmas recipe from generation to generation. These little and big traditions shape who we are and who we become.

The 'passage' in rites of passage simply means transitioning, or passing, from one stage of life to another. It can be from childhood to adulthood, from single to married, from married to divorced. From living to death. These are historical transitions that change us significantly. Sometimes we don't

NOTES

like these transitions. When we lose something we value — such as a loved one or a job — we experience unpleasant, painful feelings that impact our moods, behaviours, thoughts and general wellbeing.

Whether we like the transitions or not, it is very important to acknowledge them with a rite of passage — something to tangibly mark the change. This helps us accept the change and is the first step towards obtaining peace while in transition, so we do not live in denial.

In today's way of living, we may think that traditions are outdated and no longer as important as they used to be. However, many traditions from centuries back are still important today. For instance, when a child is born, we celebrate a new life with practices passed down from generation to generation and from family to family. While the practices might be different, new life is still celebrated.

The next biggest rite of passage in our lives is usually the transition from childhood to adulthood. Different practices may take place, such as circumcision for boys. During this time, the 'uncles' talk to the boys about what is manhood and the expectations of a man in society. Similar with girls — before they start their menstrual time, or just after they have started, the 'aunties' talk to the girls about what is womanhood and how the menstrual cycle leads to changes such as sex and children. These conversations show that they are no longer children but young adults. They are leaving behind one season and beginning another. The rite of passage teaches them how to behave and reduces stigma and shame by preparing them for the changes that are starting to happen to them inside and out.

*There is a time for everything,
and a season for every activity under
the heavens:
a time to be born and a time to die,
a time to plant and a time to uproot,
a time to kill and a time to heal,
a time to tear down and a time to
build,*

a time to weep and a time to laugh,
a time to mourn and a time to dance,
a time to scatter stones and a time to gather them,
a time to embrace and a time to refrain from embracing,
a time to search and a time to give up,
a time to keep and a time to throw away,
a time to tear and a time to mend,
a time to be silent and a time to speak,
a time to love and a time to hate,
a time for war and a time for peace.

Ecclesiastes 3:1–8

Denying the existence of these rites of passage is like denying the very cycle of life. Each culture has different practices to mark our many rites of passage, but they all share a common factor in doing *something* to mark our passages. Not acknowledging the different seasons we are in — it's like denying our existence! This is true also for challenging seasons. When we are in a season of loss and do not acknowledge it, we live in denial of self. Although it is painful to do so, we need to accept and acknowledge the feelings of losing someone or something.

Loss is one of the most painful experiences anyone can ever go through. It leaves us questioning our identity, what we believe in and what we stand for. We may question everything in our lives to the point that nothing makes sense anymore.

When nothing makes sense, we often start doing things out of character. We may try to excessively please others in order to fill the void of loss. But this usually leaves us feeling remorse and guilt. For a little while, we may convince ourselves that it's okay and we've got this. Yet keeping up this persona drains us from who we are and the goodness that we carry.

Why, my soul, are you downcast?
Why so disturbed within me?
Put your hope in God,
for I will yet praise him,
my Savior and my God.

Psalm 42:11

When we are facing loss, we often come back to the same thought pattern: *Why is this happening to me* or *Why did this happen to me? Where did I go wrong? I might be the reason to be blamed.* Let's say we lose a close relationship. We might start to wonder, *Am I good enough? Why did God let this happen?* or *Why do bad things always happen to me?* We wanted that relationship to last, so we become angry and ask God *why*. Why did we have to lose that relationship, that person we loved?

But as flawed humans, we sometimes want things that are not good for us. God sees things that we don't see. God hears conversations that we can't hear. God knows the end from the beginning. We may not understand in that moment. It could be that the relationship had stopped glorifying God, had prevented self-growth or was unhealthy. We may go for days and weeks dwelling on the loss of something that had been preventing us from growth, something that had actually been bringing sorrow into our lives. Perhaps loss is God giving us the grace to embrace change and learn to be better.

Our part is to acknowledge when the season we are in has ended and that it is time to go through a rite of passage and begin the new season that God is ushering us into. What we had before may no longer gives us true purpose, so it had to go. Realising this truth not only empowers us but also liberates us. Understanding that what we lost did not lead us in the right direction helps us to be firm in who we are and be ready for the next season. Although it's difficult to seek light at the end of the tunnel, making the bold move of accepting a loss really means choosing to trust in God's sovereignty when we are surrounded by darkness.

"Don't call me Naomi," she told them. "Call me Mara, because the Almighty has made my life very bitter. I went away full, but the Lord has brought me back empty. Why call me Naomi? The Lord has afflicted me; the

LOSS

Almighty has brought misfortune upon me."

Ruth 1:20–21

Sometimes we can be like Naomi, unable to see that our loss is leading us to greater blessings. We need to trust in God's process, even though we may stumble, and move towards a total surrender to Him who owns the whole universe and whose love and mercies are endless. When we lean on God, we hear His truth — that He loves us abundantly. And we get to see His love and mercy anew all day every day.

Often God works on us and in us when we experience a loss: when we

NOTES

have lost a job, a loved one, a special place or even a dream. Loss brings up difficult emotions, which allow our character to be shaped. The question is, shaped into what? When we trust God and let Him shape our character, we discover the truth of who we are. We break free from the false narrative that the world speaks, the false identity that we wore on our sleeves and the misconceptions of truths that we believed in. We continue believing in the world's narratives until we trust God through loss and let Him heal us by first removing the old thinking patterns.

When we experience loss, we may feel that the loss is not meant to be in our lives and that what we had was an important part of who we are. When we believe this, the loss cripples us, makes us doubt, steals our peace and joy and takes away our positive feelings or experiences — all while other people think you've got it all. The loss makes you think that you are unlucky and have nothing to live for or offer. Not realising that God is simply preparing you for your next chapter in life.

As written in Jeremiah 1:5, before we were formed in our mother's womb, God knew us. He knows our past, He knows our present and He knows our future. Which means that whatever we are going through in life, He is with us. Knowing this, we can learn to trust in God's understanding and not our own limited understanding, which makes us doubt His timing.

In due time, God leads us towards healing and restoration. Then our loss becomes our joy because we see that it is the doorway into a new life and deeper understanding of God's great love.

Prayer of loss

Dear heavenly Father,

Thank you for the gift of life. Thank you for watching over me and for watching over my loved ones. I'm grateful for everything that You have done for me and given me.

During this difficult and challenging time, I pray that You shine Your face upon my life, giving me the strength I need to carry on. Father, You know what's best for me — more than I know myself. You are the one who gives and takes away. Help me trust that this loss is part of Your good and loving plan.

Amen.

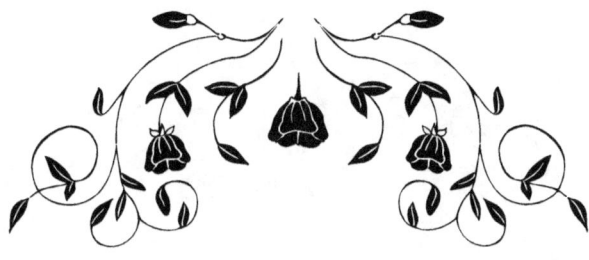

GRIEF

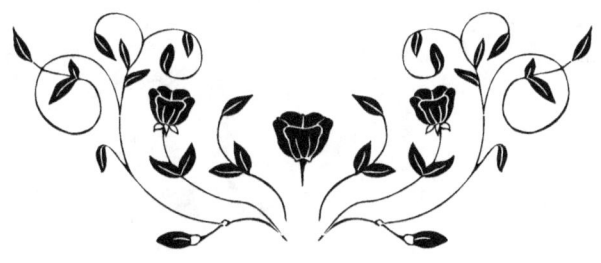

GRIEF

Grief is an intense sorrow associated with feelings of hurt, pain, heaviness and disappointment. We have all experienced grief in one way or another. Perhaps we lost a loved one in death or lost something of significant value such as a house, car, job or an opportunity. We might lose a relationship and then start feeling guilty, ashamed, embarrassed and stupid for trusting someone's words instead of our intuition.

As much as these experiences might be painful and uncomfortable, we must acknowledge that they are a part of our life's journey. Each and every stage of life is important and beneficial to us in one way or another. Each situation serves a purpose —

NOTES

as a lesson or as an experience. We either learn from the lessons or they will keep recurring until we allow them to teach us something.

Though he slay me, yet will I hope in him;
I will surely defend my ways to his face.

Job 13:15

Many of us have experienced traumatic events while growing up or at a particular time in our lives. These events can hinder our growth and development into the people God intended us to be. When we are not the people God wills us to be, we don't always react well to the things that God has put in front of us. It may take longer to accomplish our achievements, but we will get there because God does not abandon us. He is with us on the mountain top and He is with us in the valley.

While grief is an important emotion to experience, the key is in knowing when to stop grieving and start healing. Grief is a journey we move through, not a destination we stay in. Long periods of grieving can cause depression, anxiety and other emotional turmoil that may be even more difficult to overcome. This can cause resentment, bitterness and hatred in our hearts. No matter what we do, we don't feel any positive emotions, and we have nothing to

NOTES

look forwards in our world. We may want to cry out like this psalmist:

*Surely in vain I have kept my
heart pure
and have washed my hands in
innocence.
All day long I have been afflicted,
and every morning brings new
punishments.*

Psalm 73:13–14

But if we stop there, we miss the revelation that follows:

*When my heart was grieved
and my spirit embittered,
I was senseless and ignorant;
I was a brute beast before you.*

Yet I am always with you;
you hold me by my right hand.
You guide me with your counsel,
and afterward you will take me
into glory.
Whom have I in heaven but you?
And earth has nothing I desire
besides you.
My flesh and my heart may fail,
but God is the strength of my heart
and my portion forever.

Psalm 73:21–26

Grief may also affect our relationships with everyone around us. The longer the grieving process is, the more we withdraw from our loved ones, our lives and our realities. This isolation causes us to shift into survival mode and prevents us from experiencing positive feelings or the presence of God. We start losing our identity and sense of meaning. We start regretting, resenting and blaming ourselves for the loss we are enduring.

When we stay in grief, these strong emotions can create an environment that is not sustainable for our growth in Christ. This environment hinders our growth, as we may take up a skewed identity — who we think we are rather than who God intends us to be. When we follow a skewed identity, we start getting into the wrong relationships, we start doing things out of character, we make the wrong decisions, and we feel guilt and shame due to our inability to function better. This can take a toll on our general wellbeing and leave us feeling overwhelmed by the mere memory of losing the person or thing that was important to us.

We begin our journey through grief by accepting things as they are. One way of doing this is by journaling. Writing about our feelings and our thoughts can be helpful, as it's a form of releasing and allows us to see our thoughts in words. This can be the starting point for healing.

Another way is meditation, which helps with being grounded. Being grounded clears our thoughts and lets us be in tune with our bodies. Acknowledging our feelings through meditation helps us to find the core issue that is deep down in our hearts. We sit with our feelings until we can identify them, and we ask for God's guidance on how to take the next step in our journey of grief.

God understands our journey of grief and He provides for us each step of the way. We just need to listen to Him and keep walking through the dark valley.

The Lord is my shepherd, I lack nothing.
He makes me lie down in green pastures,
he leads me beside quiet waters,
he refreshes my soul.
He guides me along the right paths
for his name's sake.
Even though I walk

GRIEF

through the darkest valley,
I will fear no evil,
for you are with me;
your rod and your staff,
they comfort me.

You prepare a table before me
in the presence of my enemies.
You anoint my head with oil;
my cup overflows.
Surely your goodness and love will
follow me
all the days of my life,
and I will dwell in the house of the
Lord forever.

Psalm 23

During our grief journey, we may be able to look back on the loss with a

NOTES

clear mind and realise that what we lost was not always so good. Sometimes this realisation brings its own challenges. We may reminisce on the past and feel ashamed. Wishing that we could have done something differently, or asking ourselves what we could change if we went back in time. Then we get stuck in the past.

Given that we experienced the past, we know how it went. We live in the present, so we see how it is going. But we have no idea what will happen in the future. Often we get stuck in the past that we know to try and escape the future of unknowns. To pull ourselves out of the past, we need to learn to forgive ourselves and let go. We need to surrender to God, the only one who brings the dead to life and can make dry things green again.

By leaning on God's protection and direction, we realign our purpose with His will for our lives. The more we align with God's will, the better our decisions get and the easier our lives are. We can do this through daily prayers and devotion, fasting, going to therapy or connecting with our inner child whom God created. By reflecting on who we truly are, we tune ourselves to God's Spirit and can hear His will in our intuition. From this, we can be assertive in our discernment and make decisions that are for us and not against us.

Love and comfort are important ingredients for our grief journey. The first place to seek these is within. We do this by aligning with God's will, accepting that we are grieving and making peace with our feelings and emotions. Our next step is a commitment to bring our inward understanding outward. To some, this can be starting to get out of bed, trying to eat something or taking a shower. To another, it can be writing a thank you or a goodbye letter to whom or what we are grieving for.

Praise be to the God and Father of our Lord Jesus Christ, the Father of compassion and the God of all comfort, who comforts us in all our troubles, so that we can comfort those in any trouble with the comfort we ourselves receive from God.

2 Corinthians 1:3–4

Another way that we seek love and comfort is through friends and family. Many of us tend to isolate ourselves when we are going through the challenges of life. Instead, we should allow people to comfort us. Letting them in and sharing our pain does not burden them. It allows us to appreciate and acknowledge their presence during our grieving season. And as we heal and discover peace and joy within us, we can share this with the people who comforted us and also with the world around us.

We should learn to not lean on our own understanding but on what God's word says about us and what He promises for life. Only then can we journey through grief and find hope, peace and healing.

in any trouble with the comfort we ourselves receive from God.

2 Corinthians 1:3–4

Another way that we seek love and comfort is through friends and family. Many of us tend to isolate ourselves when we are going through the challenges of life. Instead, we should allow people to comfort us. Letting them in and sharing our pain does not burden them. It allows us to appreciate and acknowledge their presence during our grieving season. And as we heal and discover peace and joy within us, we can share this with the people who comforted us and also with the world around us.

NOTES

We should learn to not lean on our own understanding but on what God's word says about us and what He promises for life. Only then can we journey through grief and find hope, peace and healing.

Prayer for grief

Father God,

You know my comings and my goings: nothing on this earth and in my life happens without You knowing.

Give me the grace I need to carry on and the strength I need to carry this cross You have entrusted to me.

I might not see the good in this moment, but I trust that everything You have permitted to happen is for the good of Your glory.

All I can say is, let Your will be done.

Amen

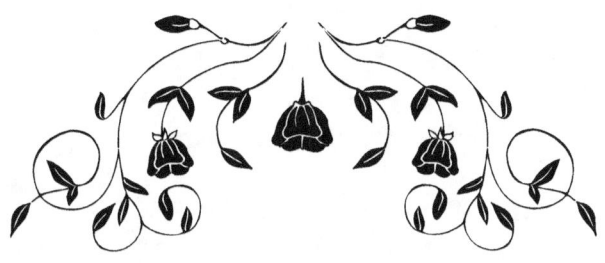

HEALING

HEALING

Healing is the process of recovery and becoming healthy again. It typically occurs after going through the stages of loss and grieving, after accepting and acknowledging our hurt and disappointment. We then begin our recovery journey by allowing all our emotions and feelings to come up and then dealing with them in a healthy and sustainable way. After healing, we may end up with a scar. But we will still gain new life and hope for a better future.

A healthy and sustainable way of healing looks different to each and every one of us. Some may go to therapy, while others may start a health and fitness journey. Perhaps we need to draw closer to God or

NOTES

participate more in activities that inspire us such as gardening, starting a new hobby or joining a new social group.

While recovering, we should remember the different types of healing: spiritual, emotional and physical. First, spiritual healing is reconnecting with our faith or religious beliefs, with God and with people in our community who practice and believe in faith. We can restore these connections via prayers, anointing oils, discipleship, worship and so on. Emotional healing is the process of acknowledging, processing and integrating painful life experiences and strong emotions. This often occurs in a therapy setting with a mental health practitioner present. Physical healing is repairing of damaged organs, tissues and the biological system as a whole. Physical healing may come about from resting, physical therapy or strength training, prescribed medication, going to the doctors and self-care.

While all three are important, I will focus on emotional and spiritual healing, as these are often the most neglected.

*He heals the brokenhearted
and binds up their wounds.*

Psalm 147:3

Emotional healing can be a deciding factor for our general wholeness and healing. In psychology, scientists often discuss how our emotions and stressors impact our quality of life. Until we heal emotionally, we are impacted by our stressors; even little reminders bring back unpleasant emotions — the same way hearing that classic shark music in a movie triggers certain emotions and images.

Healing from a relationship betrayal may take weeks or months, depending on the level of commitment and time invested with the person. While we are still healing, even hearing the word 'relationship' or seeing a couple on social media might trigger all the negative emotions and disappointment that we experienced. So the word 'relationship' becomes a stressor, and seeing someone who resembles the person who betrayed us becomes our shark music.

When triggered, we may withdraw from activities and our social life, because we feel frightened and overwhelmed by the many feelings and emotions. This leads to unhealthy coping mechanisms such as excessive drinking, shopping sprees, partying hard and toxic patterns. But we can never be satisfied nor fulfilled with the things of this world or from people, as they only impact us in that moment. And once the thrilling excitement is over, we return to our low moods, lonely minds, empty souls and the gaping void in our hearts. In the long run, unhealthy coping mechanisms often cost us so much more than the original loss we experienced. Instead of getting better, we get more hurt and disappointed and add self-inflicted injuries.

No matter how many times we have done this, we can still say enough is enough and break the cycle of unhealthy coping mechanisms. This can be done by digging deep down inside our hearts and asking, *What am I longing for? Why do I feel so much pain like this? How did I become my only enemy? How can I fill this emptiness?* When we look deep inside and name what is actually troubling us, we become free to learn a better way of coping.

HEALING

Lord my God, I called to you for help,
and you healed me.
You, Lord, brought me up from the
realm of the dead;
you spared me from going down to
the pit.

Psalm 30:2–3

Before we start our healing journey, we acknowledge that we are in pain and wounded. Our hearts are broken, we are disappointed, and we feel like there's nothing to look up to. When we allow ourselves to sit with these feelings and pay attention to what our bodies are saying, we start processing our feelings and emotions and start healing by simply being present in our lives. Engaging with

NOTES

the ideas and thoughts that come to our mind. Engaging our hearts and being kind to ourselves. We heal by accepting the things that we can't change. Even when trying to heal in a healthy way, bad days will come. But remember that God will be with you each and every step of the way.

The Lord makes firm the steps
of the one who delights in him;
though he may stumble, he will not
fall,
for the Lord upholds him with
his hand.

Psalm 37:23–24

Healing also involves acknowledging if we played a role in the loss. For example, healing from a relationship breakdown may mean recognising that we rushed into a relationship without getting to know the person better or that we settled for a one-sided relationship. Reflecting on our part played in the loss may reveal underlying issues that we need to face in order to become whom God intends us to be. This can be a major breakthrough for our healing.

For spiritual healing, we reconnect with God and His great love through forgiveness. We heal by learning to forgive ourselves for our role played in being hurt, wounded and broken. We heal by also not holding grudges with the people who hurt us, but by forgiving them and releasing them.

This cannot be done by trying to force ourselves to forget or get over someone or something that has hurt us. Instead, we should acknowledge the pain associated with the person or the event as it comes to our mind and release it over and over again, until remembering the person or the events that have hurt us doesn't damage our general wellbeing.

For if you forgive other people when they sin against you, your heavenly Father will also forgive you.

Matthew 6:14

Whenever a person who hurt us comes to mind, pray for them. Wish them well and pray for God to bless them, protect them and for God to help them become the person He created them to be. This is a big step for anyone to take in terms of forgiveness and healing, but it's the easiest way to make peace with ourselves and to stop resenting people who have hurt us. Not forgiving and releasing who or what hurt us can make us bitter, which robs us of the peace and joy that Christ has for us in our lives. Thus, it is important that every single time we think of someone who hurt us, we should always say *I forgive you* and mention their name.

Healing is the only way to experience a happy and healthy life. When we don't heal, our decisions are impacted

NOTES

by our residual grief and pain. And this hinders us from living our lives to the fullest. By choosing to engage in healing, we find self-love and practice self-compassion. And once we heal, we naturally seek things that are better for ourselves and seek environments that will nurture us.

Prayer for healing
Lord God,

I come before you in my sinful nature — wailing, hurt and broken. I pray that you heal my mind, body and soul.

As you healed the ten leapers, don't forget me. As you healed the woman with the issue of blood, heal my brokenness and my pain.

If only I can touch the hem of your garment, I will be made whole. Father, only say the word and my soul shall be healed.

Amen.

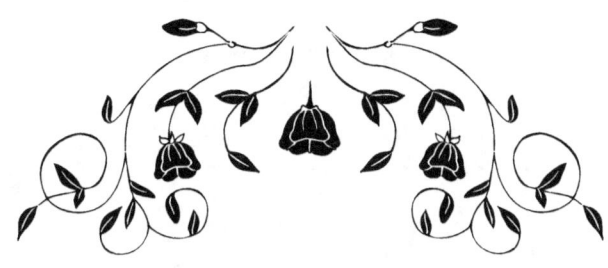

SELF-ACCEPTANCE

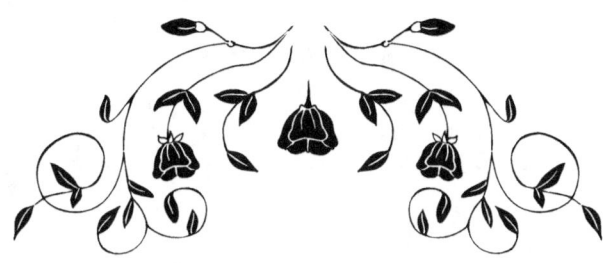

SELF-ACCEPTANCE

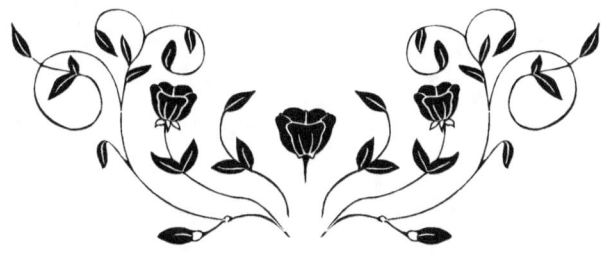

SELF-ACCEPTANCE

Self-acceptance is when an individual accepts all of their attributes, both negative and positive. In other words, accepting all of you as you are, both the good and the bad. Some people may think, *Of course who doesn't accept themselves?* But, unfortunately, many of us struggle with this.

It is hard to accept some parts of ourselves. Such as the part that criticises others, that envies others, that struggles with self-confidence. Or the part of us that feels inadequate, that self-criticises, that hates physical parts of our body. Perhaps we have a part that is filled with regret, that self-sabotages, that believes we deserve the betrayals and rejections that we have encountered.

NOTES

These parts don't represent our true identity. They were imparted onto us by the world from the experiences we have been through such as rejection, denial, shame and feeling like we are not good enough. We should instead lean into whom God created us to be before our identity took on parts from the world.

For you created my inmost being; you knit me together in my mother's womb.

Psalm 139:13

Our perception of self and who we are is often influenced by our environment and surroundings. But God says, *Before I formed you in the womb*

SELF-ACCEPTANCE

I knew you (Jer 1:5). God gave us our true identity before the world started to taint us, before we were taught to react to challenges with fear and pain and doubt. If we keep agreeing and accepting our worldly identities, we make choices that reinforce this false self-narrative. We make wrong decisions based on who we think we are. We choose the wrong friends, we love the wrong people, we stay in the wrong environments, and we work in the wrong jobs.

Deep inside us, we know that we want better and that we can do better. This is our true identity crying out. But we are often ridden by guilt and shame, so we keep punishing ourselves for the wrong decisions that we have

NOTES

made. We struggle to accept ourselves and to love ourselves as we are because we feel unworthy of our true identity. This can lead to settling into poor relationships or work situations and giving people permission to mistreat us — while knowing deep down that we deserve to be treated with dignity and respect. Not knowing who God designed us to be and accepting the world's narrative of who we are makes us settle for less and think we belong in the clearance rack.

We need to wake up in the morning, look at ourselves in the mirror and speak truth into ourselves. Tell ourselves words that affirm our true identity — the one that God created us with. He gave us the breath of life

SELF-ACCEPTANCE

into our nostrils. We are wonderfully and fearfully made by a loving God. Our eyes resemble God, our hands, our hearts, our toes, our feet, our legs, our arms, each and every part of our bodies and our beings are gifts from the Almighty God who created the Heavens and the Earth.

When we don't like parts of our bodies or who we are, it's like we are saying that God made a mistake in creating us as we are — which is distressing, because we know very well that God does not make mistakes. In truth, the parts of ourselves that we are ashamed of, that we think are a mistake, are false narratives given to us by the world.

NOTES

> *For I know the plans I have for you," declares the Lord, "plans to prosper you and not to harm you, plans to give you hope and a future. Then you will call on me and come and pray to me, and I will listen to you. You will seek me and find me when you seek me with all your heart. I will be found by you," declares the Lord, "and will bring you back from captivity.*
>
> *Jeremiah 29:11–14*

Although we will make mistakes and later realise we should have done something better, we should make peace with our past decisions. Often the decisions we made were based on the information we had at that particular moment. But even when we have more information, we can still make mistakes. We may assume that if we know better, we do better. However, it is not that simple. We might have a wealth of wisdom, but if it is not used properly, it can lead to our detriment.

For instance, our past experiences can cloud our judgement. When faced with an obstacle similar to one we have faced before, a memory of fear might drive us to shrink and make decisions based on our past hurt rather than on the moment. Even if we have faced a similar situation before, it won't always have the same outcome. While we are wiser by our past experiences, we should not be bound by them. We should strive to live in the moment for the moment.

You have searched me, Lord,
and you know me.
You know when I sit and when I rise;
you perceive my thoughts from afar.
You discern my going out and my
lying down;
you are familiar with all my ways.
Before a word is on my tongue
you, Lord, know it completely.
You hem me in behind and before,
and you lay your hand upon me.

Psalm 139:1–5

What should we do with our painful experiences and memories? They become our strength. Our scars are

SELF-ACCEPTANCE

our victory signs, proof that we have fought a good fight and that we trust that we will become victorious at the end of the tunnel. Every moment of pain can become a well of strength to draw from when we face new challenges and difficult moments. We should always remember where we've come from and what we've overcome.

Not only so, but we also glory in our sufferings, because we know that suffering produces perseverance; perseverance, character; and character, hope. And hope does not put us to shame, because God's love has been poured out into our hearts through the Holy Spirit, who has been given to us.

Romans 5:3–5

NOTES

In all circumstances, God has already gone before us and knows the challenges we are facing. He knows the end from the beginning. He knows our being and our exact reaction at every moment. And even if we make mistakes in the future, God already knows this and has planned for it — and He has already forgiven us for it! In all things, He goes before us, and He orders our steps according to His mighty will and abundant love. With this truth, we have the strength to welcome new life.

Prayer for self-acceptance

Dear Lord,

Even before you created me in my mother's womb, you knew me.

You know my coming, You know my going, You know my being, You know my strength — and You know my weakness. Father, I trust when You said the plans You have for me are to prosper me and not to harm. Give me the strength I need when I face challenges and, through these trials, reveal the identity You crafted within me.

Thank You for loving me and thank you for accepting all of me — my good, my bad and my ugly. I glorify You, Lord, with all of my being.

Amen

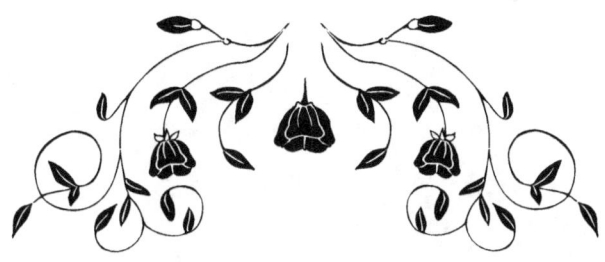

LIVING LIFE

What do we mean by 'life'? I would say life is how, when and where we live. The environments we inhabit impact the quality of life we can have. This includes our work environment, religious environment and social environment.

In all these environments, we meet people. Each person whose path we cross impacts our lives in one way or another. We may have a positive life experience or discover a lesson we need to learn. The people whose paths we cross can affect the type of day we have. *We may say Today I had a good day* or *I'm having a bad day*. What we usually mean is that our day has been affected by the experiences we have encountered — good or bad.

NOTES

We all understand and relate to having good days and bad days. We all share in knowing painful lived experiences such as loss, grief and feeling sad or lonely. Even if we use the same word for these emotions and experience them in a similar way, the experiences and what triggers the emotions are different.

Some days can't be described with just 'good' or 'bad'. If we ever go through traumatic or life-changing moments, we may feel lost for words. However, finding ways to speak about our experiences is important to help others understand our journey and relate to us.

But the big question is, how do we live a normal life after we have been through life-altering moments? A big part of living life in this world is how we manage the not-so-good days we encounter. As much as we like to think that living life is easy, one traumatic experience can break our normal cycle of life and make easy things hard. This normal cycle is different for each person, depending on their circumstances and the environment they grew up in.

Do not conform to the pattern of this world, but be transformed by the renewing of your mind. Then you will be able to test and approve what God's will is—his good, pleasing and perfect will.

Romans 12:2

Learning to live life again and find our normal cycle after encountering a life-changing moment can be challenging. And it looks different for different people and different experiences. Depending on the level of injuries and trauma, recovery may take a long time and things getting back to a normal way of living may take even longer.

For example, imagine we have three passengers in a car crash. Passenger one sustains minor scrapes and bruises; passenger two sustains moderate injuries, with a strained neck and a broken leg; and passenger three sustains life-threatening injuries that put them in a coma and paralyse them from the waist down. Each passenger's recovery time includes not only the initial care and treatment to heal their bodies but also the modification of their homes and time to learn how to live each day of their new normal cycle. Getting used to their new reality will be difficult and adjusting to their new lives will be even harder.

In him we were also chosen, having been predestined according to the plan of him who works out everything in conformity with the purpose of his will, in order that we, who were the first to put our hope in Christ, might be for the praise of his glory.

Ephesians 1:11–12

But the impact of the accident can be even greater than we first realise. In addition to physical pain and healing, the victims and their loved ones may also face emotional pain and healing. For example, while passenger one sustained minor injuries, the emotional toll from being involved in an accident might be difficult to bear; they may develop fears of ever driving or sitting in a car seat. On the other hand, passenger two might take a bit longer to recover physically, but emotionally they might be less affected than all the other passengers.

This means that with the right treatment and care, passenger two makes a full recovery first. It will still take some time to get their life back to normal, but they may adjust easily. Passenger three has serious physical injuries that will take a long time to heal from, and their life may never go back to how it was before. Facing the daunting journey of physical healing and learning a new normal may also cause them emotional stress and pain. This adds to their healing journey.

A person who has a physical injury or ailment is easier to notice than someone who has an emotional or psychological ailment. Treating emotional and mental wounds is often harder, as the wounds can only be identified by the person experiencing them. Because it is challenging to explain what we are experiencing, it is hard to get support for this suffering. Society and the community at large are more easily drawn to and sympathise with someone who has a physical condition that they can see compared to a person who has emotional, mental or spiritual wounds.

"What do you think? If a man owns a hundred sheep, and one of them wanders away, will he not leave the ninety-nine on the hills and go to look for the one that wandered off? And if he finds it, truly I tell you, he is happier about that one sheep than about the ninety-nine that did not wander off. In the same way your

Father in heaven is not willing that any of these little ones should perish.

Matthew 18:12–14

The injuries from a traumatic event may not be present at first, but the aftermath is felt for years to come. That's why each person's journey and experiences are unique. As much as we might have similar life experiences, our emotions and feelings are unique to each person. This helps to explain why the remedy or the tools that work for one may not work for another. All we can do is accept who we are and where we are and try to personalise our recovery based on our individual needs. That may be going to therapy, learning how to drive again, learning how to walk again or a combination.

When healing from non-physical injuries, therapy alone may not be the answer — we also lean on our faith. God is the absolute healer, who makes all things new and work for our good.

You intended to harm me, but God intended it for good to accomplish what is now being done, the saving of many lives.

Genesis 50:20

What could have been orchestrated to destroy you can be the stepping stone of your destiny. There's a common saying, 'where there's a will, there's a way'. As long as we lean not on our own understanding and learn to trust in God's providence, He will always make a way where there seems to be none.

Living life and learning a new normal cycle after life-altering moments is like learning how to ride a bicycle. We will hop on the bicycle, fall, rise again and fall again. The more we practice how to ride the bicycle, the better we get. Such is recovery after experiencing traumatic events. We cannot just recover and forget what we have been through. Rather, we learn to gradually get better and better in coping and dealing with life's hardest moments. And so what once

NOTES

knocked us out may not cause the same negative impact next time. We get better at solving conflicts, at dealing with difficult emotions, and we develop better coping mechanisms. Our God says:

"Come to me, all you who are weary and burdened, and I will give you rest. Take my yoke upon you and learn from me, for I am gentle and humble in heart, and you will find rest for your souls. For my yoke is easy and my burden is light."

Matthew 11:28–30

Only through God can we learn to live the life that He designed and enjoy it to the fullest.

Prayer for living life

Dear heavenly Father,

I pray that You continue to look after me, my family and friends, and that You ordain each and every step we take.

May You protect us, guide us, nourish us and look after us through this life that is full of ups and downs and moments we can't predict. We trust You, for You know what's best for us.

May all that I am be for Your Glory.
May I become whom I ought to be for Your Glory.
God, the author and finisher.

May You continue to cover us O Lord Jesus Christ with Your precious blood each moment we live, and may we live to glorify Your name.

Amen.

About The Author

Fotina was born in a country of a thousand hills called Rwanda and was raised in Kenya.

As a refugee in Kenya, she grew up in the less privileged outskirts of Nairobi called Kayole, also referred to as the 'Ghetto'. Throughout this, Fotina had a normal childhood — or what seemed to be 'normal'. Years later into adulthood, she discovered the different perspectives on the term 'normal'.

She is described as an empathy burner, and it has become her life mission to bear a light for everyone who has been impacted by life-changing events that bring loss and impact our normal.

Professionally, she has worked in human services and social work for a decade, engaging with people from all walks of life and backgrounds. Fotina strives to shine a light on mental health conditions and is inspired to be a mental health champion by her lived experiences and what she has encountered through society and her professional field. She aspires to bring much-needed light into our world by lighting one candle at a time.

For more about Fotina, see her Instagram profile: @fotina_mugane.